A. E. HOUSMAN

☙

THE CONFINES OF CRITICISM

THE CAMBRIDGE INAUGURAL
1911

THE COMPLETE TEXT
WITH NOTES BY
JOHN CARTER

CAMBRIDGE
AT THE UNIVERSITY PRESS
1969

Published by the Syndics of the Cambridge University Press
Bentley House, 200 Euston Road, London N.W.1
American Branch: 32 East 57th Street, New York, N.Y.10022

© Cambridge University Press 1969

Standard Book Number: 521 07718 4

Printed in Great Britain
at the University Printing House, Cambridge
(Brooke Crutchley, University Printer)

CONTENTS

PREFACE

IN 1911 A. E. Housman, then Professor of Latin at
University College London, was elected Kennedy
Professor of Latin in the University of Cambridge
in succession to J. E. B. Mayor, who had occupied the
chair since the retirement, thirty-eight years earlier,
of its first holder, H. A. J. Munro, the foremost
English Latinist of the nineteenth century, as Housman is generally considered to be of the twentieth.

On 9 May he delivered his Inaugural Lecture in the
Senate House to what Mr A. S. F. Gow has described
as 'a crowded and curious audience'.[1] Housman, an
Oxford man, was personally new to Cambridge, and
he was known there not only as the editor of Manilius
and Juvenal and an authorative textual critic who
knew how to mix acid with his ink, but also as the
author of *A Shropshire Lad*. Henry Jackson of Trinity,
writing on the following day to Arthur Platt, Housman's closest friend at University College, reported
that:

Housman's discourse was excellent. He smote with all his
might two tendencies of modern scholarship—on the one
hand, aesthetic criticism; on the other hand, the slavish

[1] *A. E. Housman: A Sketch* (1936), p. 33.

7

mechanical methods of the Germans...He trounced Swinburne most effectively in respect of a reading of Shelley. His denunciation of the 'slave labour' of the big German–Latin Dictionary rejoiced me especially. And, personally, I was much pleased with what he said about Munro and Mayor. He was kind, just and truthful.[1]

Another Trinity scholar, J. M. Image, whose obituary notice Housman was later to contribute to *The Cambridge Review*, wrote in equally enthusiastic terms about the performance of his new colleague:

Brilliant is the only epithet—flashing and scintillating with dry humour (admirably enhanced by his solemnity of face) and 'delicious irony'. One passage where he gravely mouthed a maniac outburst of extravagant, arrogant laudation by Swinburne of a Shelley line which was too short by half a foot—the very kernel of its exquisite perfection to those who had ears to hear !—and then proceeded—'Unfortunately the MS is extant in Shelley's own hand: and the line as *he* wrote it possesses the full number of syllables'.

His enthusiasm for Munro and for the Cambridge School of Scholarship warmed my heart. His eulogies on Cambridge lips would have sounded fulsome. Coming from a Member of the rival University they sounded true and generous.

Our Press ought to print the Lecture.[2]

[1] R. St J. Parry, *Henry Jackson, O.M., A Memoir* (1926), p. 164.
[2] Image's letter, written on 9 May 1911, was addressed to the wife of his lifelong friend W. F. Smith of St John's, who had not been able to attend the lecture. It is here printed from a transcript preserved among the Housman papers.

The Cambridge Inaugural, however, was never printed in its author's lifetime;[1] unlike the *Introductory Lecture* of 1892, the brilliant paper on 'The Application of Thought to Textual Criticism' delivered to the Classical Association in 1921, and the well-known Leslie Stephen Lecture of 1933, *The Name and Nature of Poetry*.[2] The reason was that Housman, to quote Mr Gow again, 'was unable to verify a statement which it contained as to the text of Shelley's *Lament* of 1821': a statement, it was to be inferred, crucial to

[1] There are two trivial exceptions. On the opening page of *The Name and Nature of Poetry* (1933), Housman quoted from the Inaugural (delivered, as he remarked, twenty-two years earlier to a day in the same place) the passage asserting the rarity among professional scholars of the faculty of literary criticism. It will be noticed (p. 27 below) that the concluding sentence about Lessing was rewritten between 1911 and 1933; whether early or late we cannot tell, for the original manuscript of the later lecture (since 1966 in the Cambridge University Library) lacks its first two sheets of text, for the absence of which Housman, when presenting it to S. C. Roberts, offered the presumably fanciful explanation that 'probably I destroyed them as containing things too bad to read'.

On pp. lv, lvi of the additional preface to the second independent edition of Housman's text of Juvenal (first constructed for Postgate's *Corpus Poetarum Latinorum*, published in ampler form in the same year 1905, reprinted, with the additional preface, 1931) the editor, disserting on XV 7, wrote, 'I take the following remarks from the inaugural lecture which I delivered at Cambridge in 1911.' He then quoted the passage beginning 'Who was the first and chief Latin writer to use the Greek word for a cat, αἴλουρος?' and ending with the apophthegm of Solomon, which will be found on p. 41 below.

[2] All three now included in *Selected Prose*, edited by John Carter (Cambridge 1961).

some textual argument in which, as Jackson's and Image's contemporary comments testified, Swinburne was involved. This 'great obstacle', Housman himself had written in 1929 in reply to a proposal from Oxford to include the unpublished lecture in a collection of his prose works, 'is one which prevented me from letting the Cambridge press publish the inaugural lecture in 1911'. Despite strenuous efforts by the scholars of the Clarendon Press, the reference on which Housman had depended continued elusive, and the manuscript of the Inaugural was after his death destroyed in accordance with its author's instructions for his unpublished prose manuscripts. Thus, not only were Shelley and Swinburne specialists left to wonder what were the grounds, and what the argument, in this formidable critic's incursion into their preserves; readers in general, and admirers of Housman in particular, were deprived of a presumptively significant addition to the canon of his prose works.[1]

In December 1967, however, when going through a confused mass of papers which had been in storage since shortly after the death of Laurence Housman

[1] The crux was identified, Swinburne's connexion with it examined, and the results of the specialist research mobilized from Oxford summarized (by the courtesy of the Oxford University Press) in an article 'Housman, Shelley and Swinburne' contributed by the present writer to *The Times Literary Supplement* (6 September 1963).

in 1959, I found, between a sheaf of receipted bills and some crumpled pacifist leaflets from the First World War, a 29-page typescript[1] headed 'Inaugural Lecture' and, near by, the front sheet of a manila envelope endorsed in Housman's writing 'Cambridge inaugural'. These papers have since been presented to the Cambridge University Library by Mr Robert E. Symons, legatee of the A. E. Housman estate. With his authority the lecture was published in *The Times Literary Supplement* of 9 May 1968, the fifty-seventh anniversary of its delivery. In deference, however, to its author's distaste for printing any argument based on an unverified premise, the Shelley–Swinburne passage was omitted; thus necessarily leaving Housman's double-barrelled attack on tendencies in the textual scholarship of 1911 with one trigger unpulled.

During the intervening twelvemonth Mr John Sparrow and I (collaborating not for the first time in Housmanian studies) resumed the quest abandoned at Oxford in 1930. The results[2] of some further research among Shelley's manuscripts and into the textual history of his posthumously published poem, *A Lament*, decisively vindicated Housman's choice of this minor crux as an example of the 'performan-

[1] See p. 13 below for a note on the text.
[2] John Carter and John Sparrow, 'Shelley, Swinburne and Housman', *The Times Literary Supplement* (21 November 1968), pp. 1318, 1319.

ces of the literary mind when, with its facile emotions and its incapacity for self-examination, it invades the province of science'. These paragraphs, which certainly sustain Henry Jackson's use of the word 'trouncing', are now published for the first time: they will be found on pp. 31–3.

The justification for restoring them is summarized in an Appendix. No one who sat at Housman's feet, as I did at Cambridge forty years ago, will suppose that he would think this as thorough as it should be. But I believe the reader will find it convincing, and I should like to hope that Housman himself might have accorded to this first unexpurgated printing of the Cambridge Inaugural, if not his *imprimatur*, at least his *nihil obstat*.

Chelsea   JOHN CARTER
Easter 1969

NOTE ON THE TEXT

The provenance of the typed transcript from which the text is set has been given in the Preface. While there can be no question about the authority of its archetype, this transcript carries no endorsement, date, or markings other than a few corrections of literals in an unidentified hand, so that its accuracy cannot be guaranteed. It has been paragraphed, the Greek accents have been regularized, a couple of cases of dittography removed, some numerals verbalized, the missing *s* restored to the word *principles* on p. 17, and two mistranscribed letters in the quotation from Horace corrected. Otherwise it is here printed verbatim; and necessarily so, for it is the only text we have.

Beyond the heading Inaugural Lecture the typescript has no title. The decision that there must be one was not mine. It seemed to me (and still seems) more than something of a presumption to do for A. E. Housman what he had no occasion, since he never prepared this lecture for publication, to do (or not to do) for himself. But, having deferred to the decision, I discovered in myself a disinclination to defer to anyone else's preferences in such presumption; so, for better or worse, the title here given to the Cambridge Inaugural is mine.

Cambridge inaugural.

THREE HUNDRED years ago, when Bacon, in his treatise on The Advancement of Learning, set out to enumerate and classify the causes which hindered that advancement and brought learning into discredit, he professed to find the chief cause in the errors and imperfections of learned men themselves. Not, he explains, in their poverty and the meanness of their employments—for example, that the government of youth is commonly allotted to them; nor again in their manners—'that they do many times fail to observe decency and discretion in their behaviour and carriage'; but in 'those errors and vanities which have intervened amongst the studies themselves of the learned', and which make them go the wrong way to work.

Whatever the advance of learning since Bacon's day, it has not yet progressed beyond the reach of errors and imperfections; and vigilance over the mode in which we conduct our studies has not ceased to be advisable. An inaugural address is a fitting occasion for taking stock of our vanities, or at least for looking the worst of them in the face and forming resolutions

15

for their amendment. I propose today to consider two current errors, as it seems to me, of some magnitude and of opposite nature. The study of Latin is a science conversant with literature: there are therefore two ways in which it ought not to be pursued. It ought not to be pursued as if it were a science conversant with the operations of nature or with the properties of number and space, nor yet as if it were itself a branch of literature, and no science at all.

It so happens that the consideration of this subject can easily be interwoven with another theme on which it is natural and proper that I should speak today. As Horace's father, desiring to exhort his son to virtue, would set before him a pattern for imitation in flesh and blood—*unum ex iudicibus selectis obiciebat*—so I can bring in example to the aid of precept, and combine a discussion of some width and generality with the commemoration of the names of individuals. This commemoration therefore, to which I now digress, is not in all aspects a digression, but has on the contrary a near relationship to one at least of the matters which I have chosen for consideration.

The Chair of Latin in this University was founded, by his friends and disciples, to the honour of the greatest classical teacher of his century, Benjamin Hall Kennedy, on his retirement, after thirty years' service, from his memorable Headmastership of Shrewsbury School. It was held in succession by two of his pupils, and indeed it has now fallen, I might almost say, to a third, though a pupil who never saw him and whom he never saw. What first turned my mind to these studies and implanted in me a genuine liking for Greek and Latin was the gift, when I was seventeen years old, of the most delightful, at any rate to me, of all volumes of translated verse—the third edition of *Sabrinae Corolla*, having Kennedy for its chief editor and chief contributor.

The practice of translation into Greek and Latin verse is often commended, in England, upon rather unsubstantial grounds, and has an efficacy imputed to it which it does not really possess. It is no doubt one way of learning prosody, but it is certainly not the only way, and possibly not even the best; while to suppose that it will confer on its practitioners any peculiar insight into the principles of ancient metre, or even any sufficient knowledge of its laws, is a delusion, and a delusion which ought by this time to have been dispelled by the facts of history. Skill to imitate the verse of the Greeks and Romans, and skill to explore its secrets and discover its rules, have both been conspicuous features of English scholarship. But they have not been conspicuous at the same time, nor in the same persons. Of the many and important additions to our knowledge of Greek and Latin metre which were made in the eighteenth century the great majority were made by English scholars: but they were made by scholars who did not themselves write Greek and Latin verse, or who did not excel in writing it.

In the nineteenth century Greek and Latin verse was written in England, and especially in Cambridge, better than it had been written anywhere in Europe since classical antiquity itself; but meanwhile the most important additions of the nineteenth century to our knowledge of Greek and Latin were made, not in England, but in Germany. That is what history has to say about the fabulous virtues of the exercise; and indeed, quite apart from history, it stands to reason that you are not likely to discover laws of metre by composing verses in which you occasionally break those laws because you have not yet discovered them. But there was the less need for fable, because verse-translation has other titles to honour which are not simply legendary. In the first place, it has intrinsic value as a fine art. It is not one of the great arts, but it is no mere handicraft either; it is an art of the same worth and dignity as the art of engraving.

As engraving to the great art of painting, so is translation to the great art of poetry; and, like the great arts, it is itself an act of creation. And here lies its chief utility in the process of educating a scholar. Learning is in the main a passive and receptive function; but the human mind, from infancy upward, feels the impulse to create; and to indulge that im-

18

pulse, however slight the value of the creation, promotes the happiness of the creator, and so enhances
his powers and enlarges his capacities. The schoolboy
who is put to his books, whether those books are
accidence and syntax or Virgil and Homer, is further
off from heaven in one regard than the child of a few
years past who sat on the ground and made mud pies.
To make mud pies is to follow at a distance and share
in modest measure the activities of the demiurge: let
the boy, as well as the child, evoke a small world out
of a small chaos; let him also behold the work of his
hands and pronounce it, if he can, to be pretty good.
A desire to create and a pleasure in creating are often
alive and ardent in minds whose true business later
is to be not creation but criticism; and even if the
things created have small intrinsic merit, the intellectual stir and transport which produced them is not
therefore vain, and has other results than these.

The elixir of life and the philosopher's stone are not
yet discovered, but alchemy in its pursuit of them
found much treasure by the way and laid the foundation of a science; so that 'it may be compared' says
Bacon 'to the husbandman whereof Aesop makes
the fable; that, when he died, told his sons that he had
left unto them gold buried underground in his vineyard; and they digged over all the ground, and gold

they found none; but by reason of their stirring and digging the mould about the roots of their vines, they had a great vintage the year following'. I could take no better example of what I mean than the early Greek hexameters of Richard Dawes. In themselves they are almost worthless, and they swarm with errors unsparingly exposed and censured by himself. But this, till he was nearly thirty years old, was evidently, in alternation with bell-ringing at St Mary's, his favourite occupation, and its true fruits are to be found elsewhere. It set up a propitious ferment in the mind, by which its faculties were enlivened, invigorated and developed; and these compositions, no monuments to his fame, are yet stepping-stones, by which he advanced to his unique achievement and celebrity in his own proper province.

When, in 1869, this chair was first constituted, there could be no question who its first occupant should rightly be; for one man was at the same time the most eminent of Kennedy's pupils, the greatest scholar in Cambridge, and the foremost English Latinist of the century. A hundred years ago the continent learnt Greek from England, and Godfrey Hermann, Porson's chief antagonist, was also Porson's chief disciple. Half a century later the English learnt Latin from the continent, and the Prometheus who fetched us the new fire from the altars of Lachmann and Madvig and Ritschl was Hugh Munro. I do not know if the affectionate admiration felt for that name in my time is still as warm as ever among those who are addressing themselves to the study of Latin; but the history of scholarship in England must be forgotten before English Latinists can cease to remember him with gratitude and reverence, *for we are also his offspring*: every one of us may make salutation to him in the words pronounced by the senate and people over the grave of Romulus,

> O pater, o genitor, o sanguen dis oriundum,
> tu produxisti nos intra luminis oras.

Munro was not primarily himself a discoverer and inventor; it is neither on the establishment of canons nor on the purification of texts nor on the illumination of obscurities that his fame is founded. But the definition of a scholar is *vir bonus discendi peritus*, and that conception was personified in Munro. In his Lucretius he produced a work more compact of excellence than any edition of any classic which has ever been produced in England. None of our great original critics, neither Bentley not Markland, Porson nor Elmsley, has left behind him a work making any pretence to such completeness: no author of any work to be compared in completeness with Munro's has observed the same austerity in selection, eschewed so scrupulously the inessential, and applied himself with such strict attention to the proper concerns of the interpreter and critic. Nor was he only a scholar: he wrote English so well that most scholars do not know how well he wrote it; and he was surely the most entertaining controversialist that ever redeemed these studies from the reproach of dullness and dustiness. It will be a long time before England or the world beholds again the same powers in the same harmony, so much sterling stuff knit together so well, such a union of solidity and accuracy, keenness and sobriety, manly taste, exhilarating humour, and engaging pugnacity. I speak, I suppose, in the presence of some to whom he was personally known: myself I never saw him, and the Cambridge photographers either did not possess his likeness or did not think proper to sell it to an Oxford undergraduate; but I did in those days molest him with letters, and I still preserved his patient and amiable replies to the young man who never even in the dreams of youth imagined that he was one day to be the successor of his illustrious correspondent.

Most good scholars are much fonder of learning than of teaching, and to Munro the duties of his office proved uncongenial and irksome. He resigned the Chair after a tenure of three years, and in 1872 it passed to the venerable man who left it vacant only last December; a scholar who in learning, if that word is taken to mean range and thoroughness of reading, had no equal in England and no superior in Europe. To dwell on the erudition of John Mayor is not merely superfluous but presumptuous; and I will now speak rather of a characteristic on which speech perhaps is not unnecessary. It is well known and sometimes lamented that for all his amplitude of knowledge he left behind him no complete work and no work having even the air of completeness. This regret I do not share; I am much more disposed to recommend for imitation the examples of one who recognized his own bent and followed it, and whose inclinations were exactly in harmony with his talents. Many a good piece of work has been spoilt by the vain passion for completeness. A scholar designs to edit a certain author, a complete edition of whom would involve the treatment of matters to whose study the editor has not been led by his own tastes and interests, and in which he therefore is not at home. The author discourses of philosophy, and the editor is no philosopher; or the author writes in complex metres, and the editor's metrical education stopped short at Porson's canon of the final cretic. It then sometimes happens that the editor, having neither the humility to acknowledge his deficiency nor the industry or capacity to repair it, scrapes a perfunctory acquaintance with the unfamiliar subject, and treats it incompetently rather than not treat it at

23

all; so that his work, for the sake of ostensible completeness, is disfigured with puerile errors, and he himself is detected, not merely in ignorance, but in imposture.

It is the absence of any such vanity, the abstention from all misdirected effort, which redeems and even converts into merit what might else appear defective in the works of Mayor. The establishment and the interpretation of an author's text were not matters in which he took the liveliest interest nor tasks for which he felt in himself a special aptitude: his likings pointed the same way as his abilities, to the collections of illustrative material. I said while he was alive, and I shall not unsay it because he is dead, that this labour is labour bestowed upon the circumference and not the centre of the subject. But this also is work which must be done, and which no other could have done so thoroughly. 'If a man read Richardson for the story', said Johnson, 'he would hang himself'; and much the same may be said not only of Mayor's *Juvenal* but of a still more celebrated book, Lobeck's *Ajax of Sophocles*. When you have finished Lobeck's commentary you have imbibed a vast deal of information, but your knowledge and understanding of the Ajax has not proportionally increased. Lobeck himself in his preface admits that this is so; τὸ μὲν πάρεργον ἔργον ὡς ποιούμεθα. He in his commentary is not principally the critic nor the interpreter, but the grammarian; and Mayor in his is principally the antiquarian and the lexicographer: his main concern is not with what the author wrote or meant, but with the words he used and the things he mentioned. These he carried in his mind through the whole width of his incomparable reading, and brought back from the limits of the literature all the parallels and imitations and echoes which it contained. What he has bequeathed us is less an edition than a treasure of subsidies: there he saw his true business, and to that business he stuck: and 'it is an uncontrolled truth', says Swift, 'that no man ever made an ill figure who understood his own talents, nor a good one who mistook them'.

These three scholars, Kennedy, Munro, and Mayor, were typical examples of what was known in the middle of the nineteenth century as Cambridge scholarship. The distinction which then existed between scholarship of the Cambridge and the Oxford type was one which did not arise till the century was in its second quarter; for scholarship meant to Elmsley what it meant to Dobree. By the fourth quarter of the century the distinction was fading away, and it cannot be said to exist at present. But while it existed it was this: Cambridge scholarship simply meant scholarship with no nonsense about it;

Oxford scholarship embodied one of those erroneous tendencies against which I take up my parable today. It was never confined to Oxford, and if now it has ceased to be regnant there it is not therefore extinct, but has gained in diffusion what it has lost in concentration.

Scholarship, that study of the ancient literatures for which chairs of Greek and Latin are founded, is itself a department (as I said before) not of literature but of science; and science ought to be scientific and ought not to be literary. The science, though it has works of literature for its subject, does not make its appeal to the same portion of the mind as do those works themselves. Scholarship, in short, is not literary criticism; and of the duties of a Latin Chair literary criticism forms no part.

And Professors of Latin may thank their stars that it does not; for a scholar, unless by accident, is not a literary critic. Whether the faculty of literary criticism is the best gift that heaven has in its treasuries I cannot say, but heaven seems to think so, for assuredly it is the gift most charily bestowed. Orators and poets, sages and saints and heroes, if rare in comparison with blackberries, are yet commoner than the appearance of Halley's comet; literary critics are less common. And when, once in a century, or once in two centuries, the literary critic does appear—will someone in this home of mathematics tell me what are the chances that his appearance will be made among that small number of people who possess a considerable knowledge of the Latin language? It may be said that Latin scholarship and literary criticism were united in the person of Lessing. Lessing, to be sure, was a great critic, and, though not a great scholar, was a good one; but if this purely accidental conjunction occurred so lately as the eighteenth century, it ought to be thousands of years before it occurs again. If, in spite of the doctrine of probabilities, the twentieth century is also to behold a Latin scholar who is a literary critic, all I know is that I am not he.

By a literary critic I understand a man who has things to say about literature which are both true and new. Appreciation of literature, and the ability to say things about it which are true but not new, is a much commoner endowment. That a scholar should appreciate literature is good for his own pleasure and profit; but it is none of his business to communicate that appreciation to his audience. Appreciation of literature is just as likely to be found in his audience as in him, for it has no connexion with scholarship. He has no right to presume that his own aesthetic perceptions are superior to those of anyone whom he addresses, or that in this respect he is better qualified to teach them than they to teach him. It is unfortunately true that audiences in general are fond of being told what they know already, and that the desire of most readers and hearers is not to be given thoughts which are new and true, but thoughts which, whether true or false, are their own thoughts, and which they rejoice to recognize dressed up in the current variety of academic journalese, and tricked out with an assortment of popular adjectives. Present to them the literary opinions which they already hold, couched in the dialect which they believe to be good English, and sprinkled over with epithets like *delicate*, *sympathetic*, and *vital*, and you will easily persuade the great majority that they are listening to literary criticism. But not quite all: there are a few, nay in some places there are not a few, who know better; and if my tastes and talents invited me in that direction I might yet be deterred by remembering what manner of men have been accustomed to frequent this seat of learning. I do not relish the prospect of standing up and pretending to be a literary critic, when in truth I am none, before audiences which may for aught I know contain such persons as Mr Thomas Gray of Peterhouse, Mr Alfred Tennyson of Trinity, or Mr John Milton of Christ's.

Why is it that the scholar is the only man of science of whom it is ever demanded that he should display taste and feeling? Literature, the subject of his science, is surely not alone among the subjects of science in possessing aesthetic qualities and in making appeal to the emotions. The botanist and the astronomer have for their provinces two worlds of beauty and magnificence not inferior in their way to literature; but no one expects the botanist to throw up his hands and say 'how beautiful', nor the astronomer to fall down flat and say 'how magnificent': no one would praise their taste if they did perform these ceremonies, and no one calls them unappreciative pedants because they do not. Why should the scholar alone indulge in public ecstasy? why from him rather than from them is aesthetic comment to be demanded? why may not he stick to his last as well as they? To be sure, we are all told in our childhood a story of Linnaeus—how, coming suddenly on a heath covered with gorse in blossom, he fell upon his knees and gave thanks to the creator. But when Linnaeus behaved in that way, he was out for a holiday: during office hours he attended to business. If Linnaeus had spent his life in genuflexions before flowering shrubs, the classification of the vegetable kingdom would have been carried out by someone else, and neither Linnaeus himself nor this popular and edifying anecdote would ever have been heard of.

Or take astronomy. If there is one sight more than another which man has been wont to regard with admiration and awe, it is the starry heavens; and these emotions are natural, just, and wholesome. If therefore you like to go out on a clear night and lift up your eyes to the stars, surrender yourself to the sentiment or meditation which they inspire, and repeat, as your choice may determine, the poetry which they have evoked from Homer or David, from Milton or Leopardi—do so by all means. But don't call it astronomy. Call it what it really is: recreation. The largest and brightest orbs of those same heavens form the subject of the third book of Newton's *Principia*; and the tenour of Newton's discourse is after this fashion:

Let S represent the sun, T the earth, P the moon, CADB the moon's orbit. In SP take SK equal to ST, and let SL be to SK in the duplicate proportion of SK to SP; draw LM parallel to PT; and if ST or SK is supposed to represent the *accelerated* force of gravity of the *earth* towards the sun, SL will represent the *accelerative* force of gravity of the *moon* towards the sun.

That is how scholars should write about literature. If the botanist and the astronomer can go soberly about their business, unseduced by the beauties of the field and unbewildered by the glories of the firmament, let the scholar amidst the masterpieces of literature maintain the same coolness of head, and let his hearers and readers allow him to exhibit the same propriety of demeanour.

In saying this, I do not depreciate the literary faculty: on the contrary, I wish to see it indulged in a sphere where it will not encounter hindrance. If you are literary, produce literature: pour the stream along its proper channel, and do not let it soak into the surrounding soil, where it will only create a quagmire. Literature is so alien from science that the literary temper in himself is a peril against which the scholar must stand on his guard. The aim of science is the discovery of the truth, while the aim of literature is the production of pleasure; and the two aims are not merely distinct but often incompatible, so that large departments of literature are also departments of lying. Not only so, but man is generally more of a pleasure-seeker than a truth-seeker, and the literary spirit, if once admitted to communication with the scientific, will ever tend to encroach upon its domain. I will give a single and signal example of this usurpation.

Among Shelley's poems of the year 1821 there is a famous and beautiful lyric, entitled *A Lament*, which was printed, and is known by heart to hundreds of thousands, in this form.

> O world! O life! O time!
> On whose last steps I climb,
> Trembling at that where I had stood before,—
> When will return the glory of your prime?
> No more, oh never more!
>
> Out of the day and night
> A joy has taken flight:
> Fresh Spring, and Summer, and Winter hoar
> Move my faint heart with grief,—but with delight
> No more, oh never more.

Against the third line of the second stanza there lie two objections, which you may call, as you please, scientific or pedantic: it has nine syllables instead of ten, and it mentions three seasons instead of four. To repair these deficiencies Mr William Rossetti in his edition of 1870(?) substituted *Autumn* for the second *and*:

Fresh Spring and Summer, Autumn, Winter hoar.

I may say in passing that I do not think Mr Rossetti's verse a good verse, nor worthy of Shelley; and I suppose that when Mr Swinburne in his *Essays and Studies* spoke of Mr Rossetti's deaf and desperate daring, he was expressing, in nobler language, the same opinion. But that is not the present point: the point is that Mr Swinburne took up the defence of the traditional text as follows:

If there is one verse in Shelley or in English of more divine and sovereign sweetness than any other, it is that in the *Lament*,

Fresh Spring, and Summer, and Winter hoar.

The music of this line taken with its context—the melodious effect of its exquisite inequality—I should have thought was a thing to thrill the veins and draw tears to the eyes of all men whose ears were not closed against all harmony by some denser and less removable obstruction than shut out the song of the Sirens from the hearing of the crew of Ulysses.

Now suppose the story ended there. How confidently, with what a depth and warmth of inward conviction, would Shelley's countrymen believe that Shelley wrote and designed to write the defective verse. How eagerly, with the sanction and encouragement of another poet so eminent as Mr Swinburne, would they give the rein to their natural inclinations and revel in the melodious effect of its exquisite inequality. But Shelley's MS exists; and the inequality, though exquisite, does not exist in Shelley's MS. Shelley wrote with his own hand

Fresh Spring and Autumn, Summer and Winter hoar
Move my faint heart with grief.

The one verse, in Shelley and in English, of more divine and sovereign sweetness than any other is the verse, not of Shelley, but of a compositor. Mr Swinburne's veins were thrilled, and tears were drawn to Mr Swinburne's eyes, by a misprint.

These are the performances of the literary mind when, with its facile emotions and its incapacity for self-examination, it invades the province of science, and allows mere prejudice in favour of the familiar to put on the air of an aesthetic judgment. And if these things are done in the green tree, what shall be done in the dry? Mr Swinburne was Shelley's compatriot, not fifty years removed from him in date, like him a poet, like him a lyrist, and indeed, in the general estimation, the authentic heir and successor of Shelley in that field of poetry. What value shall we attach to similar judgments pronounced by men who are not themselves men of letters, but merely scholars with a literary taint, on disputed passages in books written hundreds and thousands of years ago by an alien race amidst an alien culture?

When Horace is reported to have said *seu mobilibus ueris inhorruit adventus foliis,* and when pedants like Bentley and Munro object that the phrase is unsuitable to its context, of what avail is it to be assured by persons of taste—that is to say persons of British taste, Victorian taste, and sub-Tennysonian taste—that these are exquisite lines? Exquisite to whom? Consider the mutations of opinion, the reversals of literary judgment, which this one small island has witnessed in the last 150 years: what is the likelihood that your notions or your contemporaries' notions of the exquisite are those of a foreigner who wrote for foreigners two millenniums ago? And for what foreigners? For the Romans, for men whose religion you disbelieve, whose chief institution you abominate, whose manners you do not like to talk about, but whose literary tastes, you flatter yourself, were identical with yours. No: in this aspect we must learn to say of our tastes what Isaiah says of our righteousnesses: they are as filthy rags.

Our first task is to get rid of them, and to acquire,

if we can, by humility and self-repression, the tastes of the classics; not to come stamping into the library of Apollo on the Palatine without so much as wiping our shoes on the doormat, and cover the floor with the print of feet which have waded through the miry clay of the nineteenth century into the horrible pit of the twentieth. It is not to be supposed that this age, because it happens to be ours, has been specially endowed with a gift denied to all other modern ages; that we, by nature or by miracle, have mental affinity with the ancients, or that we can lightly acquire it, or that we can even acquire it at all. Communion with the ancients is purchasable at no cheaper rate than the kingdom of heaven; we must be born again. But to be born again is a process exceedingly repugnant to all right-minded Englishmen. I believe they think it improper, and they have a strong and well-grounded suspicion that it is arduous. They would much rather retain the prevalent opinion that the secret of the classical spirit is open to anyone who has a fervent admiration for the second-best parts of Tennyson.

But if in England the scholar's besetting sin is the literary attitude, or the attitude which passes for literary, the case is different in that other country, whose name can never be omitted from a survey of the condition of learning. For the past hundred years the study of the classics has had its centre in Germany, and in most departments of that study it was to Germany that Europe still looked for leadership some thirty or forty years ago. That Europe looks thither no longer is one of the many fruits of the diplomacy of Bismarck. On the battlefield of Sedan you may set up the gravestone not of one empire but of two; for where the military predominance of France fell down and perished, there also the intellectual predominance of Germany received a wound of which it bled slowly to death. It is not in classical study alone, but I hear the same tale from all quarters: that Germany, throughout the circle of the sciences, is losing or has lost her place, because her best brains are no longer employed upon the pursuit of knowledge. The Germany which led the thought of Europe was Germany disunited and poor; her union and power and wealth now provide great careers in politics, arms, and commerce; and German capabilities— these are not my words but the words of a Chancellor of the Empire—'German capabilities', said Prince Bülow four years ago, 'have taken refuge in our industry and our army'. The superiority which Germany now retains in classical scholarship is not one of quality but of quantity.

Students of Greek and Latin are by far more numerous in Germany than in any other country, and their studies are also far more completely and efficiently organized; but the students themselves are not pre-eminent, as once they were, in the power or the will to perform intellectual operations. In those periodicals which review work upon the classics you may note a perpetual recurrence of two favourite adjectives, one the conventional sign of approval, and the other of disapprobation. The one is the German word which means *methodical*, the other is the German word which means *arbitrary*. Whenever you see a writer's practice praised as *methodisch*, you find upon investigation that he has laid down a hard and fast rule and has stuck to it through thick and thin. Whenever you see a writer's practice blamed as *willkürlich*, you find upon investigation that he has been guilty of the high crime and misdemeanour of reasoning. Now the cause of this labelling, and its purpose, are equally evident. The cause may be expressed in the words of the greatest of Germans. 'Thinking is hard,' says Goethe, 'and acting according to thought is irksome' (*Denken ist schwer, nach dem Gedachten handeln unbequem*). The purpose is to lighten this labour for minds unable to cope with it, and to make the editing of a classic as simple a matter as consulting a table of logarithms. In short, while the English fault is to confuse this study with literature, the German fault is to pretend that it is mathematics.

Aristotle, near the beginning of his *Ethics*, cautions

his readers against expecting or seeking, in any department of knowledge or inquiry, a greater degree of exactness than the subject admits: πεπαιδευμένου γάρ ἐστιν ἐπὶ τοσοῦτον τἀκριβὲς ἐπιζητεῖν καθ' ἕκαστον γένος, ἐφ' ὅσον ἡ τοῦ πράγματος φύσις ἐπιδέχεται. To require demonstration from a pleader, he says, is no less absurd than to accept mere plausibility from a mathematician: the just measure of precision is that which is conformable to the subject-matter, κατὰ τὴν ὑποκειμένην ὕλην. Now the criticism and interpretation of the classical texts is not an exact science; and to treat it as if it were is falsification. Its subject-matter is a series of phenomena which are the results of the play of the human mind; and if you want to piece these phenomena together, and reconstruct the past conditions which produced them, the last person you should send for is a formulist; you had much better send for a rat-catcher. To deal with the mutable and the evasive you want no cut and dried method; and rigid rules for a fluid matter are false rules. In fact, so soon as ever we quit the abstractions of mathematics, general rules, and indeed all generalizations whatsoever, are only feasible at the cost of some sacrifice of truth.

No two particular things are exactly alike, and the better we know them the less alike we find them: perfect knowledge, if we possessed it, would render generalization impossible. Nothing therefore is more foolish, nothing combines pedantry and thoughtlessness in a more untoward union, than solemn prating about the laws of criticism, and pious horror at their violation. A man who never violates the laws of criticism is no critic. The laws of criticism are nothing but a string of generalizations, necessarily inaccurate, which have been framed by the benevolent for the guidance, the support, and the restraint, of three classes of persons. They are leading strings for infants, they are crutches for cripples and they are strait-waistcoats for maniacs. To those three large divisions of mankind they may be unreservedly recommended; but they concern nobody else, and least of all the critic, for the critic is himself the source from which they have derived whatever validity they possess. Just as poets are said to be the fountains of grammar, so the laws of criticism are merely representations, imperfect and inadequate representations, of the practice of critics; and for a critic to set about obeying them is as if a man should try to make himself look like his own reflexion in the bowl of a spoon. The critic keeps the laws of criticism nine times out of ten, because they ought to be kept: the tenth time he breaks them, because they ought to be broken. What Diderot in his third conversation on the *Fils Naturel* says of dramatic composition is no less true and salutary here: 'Especially remember', says he, 'that there is no general principle: I do not know a single one of those that I have indicated which a man of genius cannot infringe with success.'

But to the common acceptance of this truth there is a very formidable obstacle: nothing less than the nature of man himself. 'The nature of man', says Bacon, 'doth extremely covet to have somewhat in his understanding fixed and unmovable, and as a rest and support of the mind.' Men hate to feel insecure; and a sense of security depends much less on the correctness of our opinions than on the firmness with which we hold them; so that by excluding intelligence we can often exclude discomfort. The first thing wanted is a canon of orthodoxy, and the next thing is a pope. The disciple resorts to the teacher, and the request he makes of him is not *tell me how to get rid of error* but *tell me how to get rid of doubt*. In this there is nothing new: 'as knowledges are now delivered', said Bacon 300 years ago, 'there is a kind of contract of error between the deliverer and the receiver. For he that delivereth knowledge desireth to deliver it in such form as may be best believed, and not as may be best examined; and he that receiveth knowledge desireth rather present satisfaction than expectant enquiry.' Blind followers of rules will be blind followers of masters: a pupil who has got out of the habit of thinking will take his teacher's word for gospel, and will be delighted with a state of things in which intellectual scrutiny not only ceases to be a duty but becomes an act of insubordination. How this nonsense of orthodoxy and this propensity to servitude at the present time impede the advance of learning and even set it back I will show by one simple example.

Who was the first and chief Latin writer to use the Greek word for a cat, αἴλουρος? The answer to this question can be found in many Latin dictionaries, but not in the latest and most elaborate. The five greatest universities of Germany have combined their resources to produce a *thesaurus linguae Latinae*, whose instalments, published during the last twelve years, run to 6,000 pages, and have brought it down to the letter D. The part containing *aelurus* appeared in 1902; it cites the word from Gellius, from Pelagius, and from the so-called Hyginus; but it does not cite it from the fifteenth satire of Juvenal. Here we find illustrated a theme on which historians and economists have often dwelt, the disadvantage of employing slave-labour.

In Germany in 1902 the inspired text of Juvenal was the text of Buecheler's second edition. That edition was published in the last decade of the nineteenth century, when the tide of obscurantism, now much abated, was at its height, and when the cheapest way to win applause was to reject emendations which everyone had hitherto accepted and to adopt lections from the MSS which no one had yet been able to endure. Buecheler, riding on the crest of the wave, had expelled from the text the conjecture, as it then was, *aeluros*, and restored the *caeruleos* of the MSS. That was enough for the chaingangs working at the dictionary in the ergastulum at Munich: theirs not to reason why. That every other editor for the last three centuries, and that Buecheler himself in his former edition, had printed *aeluros*, they consigned to oblivion; they provided this vast and expensive lexicon with an article on *aelurus* in which Juvenal's name did not occur.

Nine years, only nine, have elapsed. *aeluros* in Juvenal's fifteenth satire is now no longer a conjecture but the reading of an important MS. Buecheler is dead, his Juvenal has been re-edited by his most eminent pupil, who happens to be an independent thinker, and *aeluros* is back again in the text. The *thesaurus linguae Latinae*, not yet arrived at the letter E, is thus already antiquated. Now it is the common lot of such works of reference that they begin to be obsolete the day after they are published; but that damage, inflicted by the mere progress of knowledge is inevitable: what is not inevitable is this additional and superabundant damage, inflicted by the mental habits of the slave.

Everyone can figure to himself the mild inward glow of pleasure and pride which the author of this unlucky article felt while he was writing it; and the peace of mind with which he said to himself, when he went to bed that night, 'Well done, thou good and faithful servant.' This is the felicity of the house of bondage, and of the soul which is so fast in prison that it cannot get forth; which commands no outlook upon the past or the future, but believes that the fashion of the present, unlike all fashions heretofore, will endure perpetually, and that its own flimsy tabernacle of second-hand opinions is a habitation for everlasting. And not content with believing these improbable things it despises those who do not believe them, and displays to the world that stiff and self-righteous arrogance of the unthinking man which ages ago provoked this sentence from Solomon: 'the sluggard is wiser in his own conceit than seven men that can render a reason'.

Well, I have now spoken of two diverse evils, as I consider them, which you and I should do our best to avoid. But if you ask me how we are to avoid them, I must answer that I do not altogether know, and that perhaps after all we cannot. It is well enough to inculcate the duty of self-examination, but then we must also bear in mind its difficulty, and the easiness of self-deception. For self-examination the will, however sincere, is not sufficient: there needs also the faculty, and that is neither universal nor even commonly found. The mind of man, as Bacon says, 'is far from the nature of a clear and equal glass, wherein the beams of things should reflect according to their true incidence; nay, it is rather like an enchanted glass, full of superstition and imposture, if it be not delivered and reduced'. But one clue I think I can commend to you which will lead in the right direction, though not all the way. I spoke just now of servility shown towards the living; and I think it significant that this is so often found in company with lack of due veneration towards the dead. My counsel is to invert this attitude, and to think more of the dead than of the living. The dead have at any rate endured a test to which the living have not yet been subjected. If a man, fifty or a hundred years after his death, is still remembered and accounted a great man, there is a presumption in his favour which no living man can claim; and experience has taught me that it is no mere presumption. It is the dead and not the living who have most advanced our learning and science; and though their knowledge may have been superseded, there is no supersession of reason and intelligence. Clear wits and right thinking are essentially neither of today nor yesterday, but historically they are rather of yesterday than of today: and to study the greatest of the scholars of the past is to enjoy intercourse with superior minds. If our conception of scholarship and our methods of procedure are at variance with theirs, it is not indeed a certainty or a necessity that we are wrong, but it is a good working hypothesis; and we had better not abandon it till it proves untenable. Do not let us disregard our contemporaries, but let us regard our predecessors more; let us be most encouraged by their agreement, and most disquieted by their dissent.

APPENDIX: SHELLEY, SWINBURNE AND HOUSMAN

NOTE. *The following paragraphs are digested from an article by John Carter and John Sparrow published in 'The Times Literary Supplement', 21 November 1968, to which (together with an earlier article, 6 September 1963, by John Carter) the curious reader is referred for further particulars.*

The reason why Housman would not allow Cambridge in 1911 or Oxford in 1929–30 to publish his Cambridge Inaugural was given in a letter of 21 September 1929 to Charles Williams of OUP:

Not far from the beginning of this century I saw, in some literary journal I suppose, an account of an autograph, or some early impression, of Shelley's O *world, O life, O time*, in which the eighth line ran 'Fresh spring and autumn, summer and winter hoar'; and this I now cannot trace.[1]

If [he added] the erudition of you people at the Oxford Press could discover it, that would put a new face on things; though I am not sure that even then a Cambridge inaugural would properly appear under your auspices.

The standard text of this well-known poem reads as follows:

> Oh, world! oh, life! oh, time!
> On whose last steps I climb

[1] It remains untraced to this day.

Trembling at that where I had stood before;
When will return the glory of your prime?
  No more—O, never more!

Out of the day and night
A joy has taken flight;
  Fresh spring, and summer, and winter hoar,
Move my faint heart with grief, but with delight
  No more—O, never more!

Now, in every text of Shelley's poems, with one exception, since the first appearance of *A Lament* (the title is Mary Shelley's) in *Posthumous Poems*, 1824, the line in question has been printed, as above, in its familiar form: one foot shorter than the corresponding line in the poem's other stanza. The one exception was W. M. Rossetti's 1870 edition (and later reprints) of *The Poetical Works of Percy Bysshe Shelley*, where (volume II, page 274) the line appeared in the form, 'Fresh Spring, and Summer, Autumn, and[1] Winter hoar', with a note by the editor that he owed this 'indisputable emendation', which both corrects the metre and completes the sequence of the seasons, to another Shelley student of the time, Frederick Gard Fleay. In 1875, Swinburne (*Essays and Reviews*) pilloried 'this incredible outrage' in some paragraphs of such ferocious indignation that Rossetti in his 1878 edition of Shelley's poems

[1] Housman left out *and* when citing Rossetti's reading: see p. 32 above.

reverted to the accepted text, 'still entertaining nevertheless a serious suspicion that Shelley wrote, or meant to write, the line with "Autumn"'.

Oxford responded to Housman's challenge to their erudition not only by mobilizing their own resources but by enlisting the reigning Shelley experts. They first reported the Rossetti reading, Swinburne's attack on it (of which no report was in fact needed) and its withdrawal. Housman replied that 'Rossetti's is not the reading I am in search of'; as indeed it is not, for he had inserted Autumn between Summer and Winter, whereas Housman's conviction was that Shelley had put it between Spring and Summer. Later Charles Williams was able to relay the result of a resort to manuscript sources by Roger Ingpen, editor with Walter Peck of the Julian Edition of Shelley (1927–30), who had written (to Frederick Page, one of Oxford's scholarly editors):

I have examined Sir John Shelley-Rolls' MS. of 'A Lament', and in the draft of Verse 2 line 3 Shelley wrote:

Autumn[2]
(From)[1] Green spring, and (su   ), and winter hoar.

[1] Cancelled. [2] The cancelled word is heavily scored out, but *su*—— (probably *summer*) is visible—*Autumn* is written above. Shelley then fair-copied the stanza & the third line reads:

Fresh spring, and summer, and winter hoar.

To this Housman replied 'On the one hand I must thank and congratulate you, but on the other you have cooked your own goose, for Mr Ingpen's report contradicts that on which I relied'. So it does, and so was Oxford's project finally abandoned.

Ingpen's report, however, was incomplete, misleading and inaccurate. It was incomplete inasmuch as this is not, as he implied, the only MS of the poem. It was misleading in that the second version of the second stanza on the same page (123) of what is now Bodleian MS Shelley adds. e. 8 is not a 'fair copy' but merely a second draft. It was inaccurate—and crucially so—in two respects: (*a*) Ingpen, when transcribing the disputed line from the first draft (see fig. 1) failed to include a cancelled single-syllable word before *& winter hoar* (probably *gray*, but anyway some rejected thought for an adjective to be attached to the preceding *autumn*); (*b*) when transcribing from what he wrongly called the fair copy (see fig. 2), he did not indicate that it reads thus: 'Fresh spring & summer   & winter hoar', with a definite gap (10 mm. wide) in the middle of the line showing that Shelley had not yet decided what word (whether the fourth season or an epithet for the middle one of three) he would insert to finish it. It is thus evident that at this stage Shelley did not regard the eighth line as metrically complete in the form

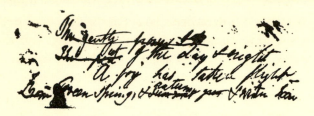

Fig. 1

Fig. 2

in which it was so highly praised (particularly for its metrical beauty) by Swinburne; the form, moreover, in which it has traditionally been printed.

The later manuscript stages, which Ingpen ignored, not only do not modify this conclusion; they powerfully reinforce it. Bodleian MS Shelley adds. e.18, p. 164, contains Shelley's own revised version (see fig. 3), made from the drafts in e.8: one of stanza I, two, as we have seen, of stanza II. In the disputed line, the empty space after *summer* is not only still there: it is decisively wider. Plainly, therefore, the poet himself regarded this eighth line as still incomplete when he copied the poem out for the last time (he died in the following year, 1822).[1]

The third MS in the Bodleian (Shelley adds. d.7, p.1) is Mary Shelley's fair copy of Shelley's last version (see fig. 4). Here, although she took liberties with the punctuation (as was her acknowledged wont), she was scrupulous in her transcription of the text itself; and that she realized that the eighth line

---

[1] It is possible that yet another MS once existed. Bodleian Shelley MS adds. d.9, which is a collection of poems copied out in Mary Shelley's hand, lacks—and already lacked when it was received from Sir John Shelley-Rolls in 1946—four leaves. Mary's index to its original contents shows that one of these leaves contained *a* poem entitled *Lament*. This title, however, was attached to other poems besides the one with which we are here concerned: for example, in this very same volume it stands above the draft of the poem beginning 'That time is dead for ever, child',

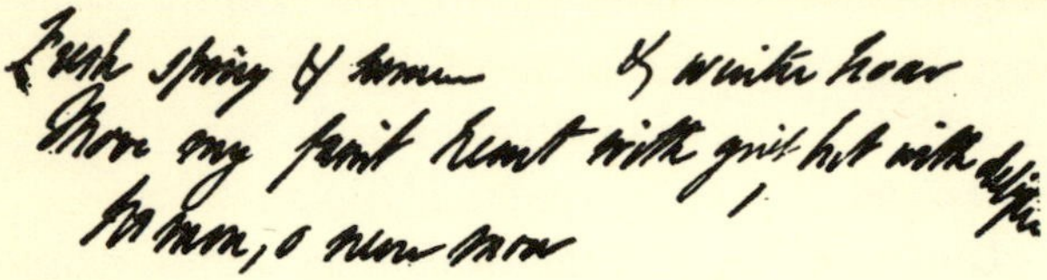

Fresh spring & summer   & winter hoar
Move my faint heart with grief, but with delight
fortune, o *new* *now*

Fig. 3

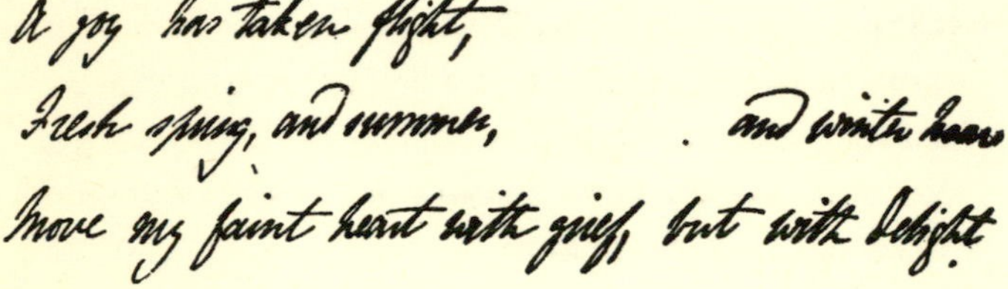

A joy has taken flight,
Fresh spring, and summer,   . and winter hoar
Move my faint heart with grief, but with delight

Fig. 4

was unfinished is emphatically indicated by the fact that she doubled the width of the open space—even though it meant crowding *hoar* right into the edge of the page.

Down to the last stage of its transition in manuscript, then, the disputed line preserved the crucial blank space: the poem was recognized as incomplete. How or why (if it was intentional) the blank was closed up for the poem's first appearance in print in 1824, to present the text in its familiar form, remains a matter of speculation. But whether or not it exactly substantiates Housman's conclusion that 'the one verse, in Shelley or in English, of more divine and sovereign sweetness than any other [he is quoting Swinburne] is the verse not of Shelley but of a compositor', the evidence of the manuscripts makes it abundantly clear that Shelley himself throughout intended a longer line, metrically matching its opposite number in the other stanza.

Housman, in short, was right, even though he could never find the evidence to prove it and therefore never published the argument. Since the gravamen of his charge against Swinburne has been vindicated, the passage that contained it may now take its proper place in the Cambridge Inaugural.